A small room is seen with a table upon which a candle burns smybolizing hospitality in welcoming of the stranger and the homeless, for in doing so, we welcome Christ Himself.

This symbol is placed fittingly in a door light at the entrance to

The First United Methodist Church of Gainesville, Ga.

BIBLICAL STAINED GLASS WINDOWS COLORING BOOK

FEATURING THE WINDOWS OF THE NARTHEX AND SANCTUARY

FIRST UNITED METHODIST CHURCH

GAINESVILLE, GEORGIA

IN MEMORY OF

REVEREND JIM THOMPSON

THIS BOOK BELONGS TO:

THE NARTHEX

VIEWED FROM INSIDE

THE ONGOING CHURCH

TOP CENTER WINDOW

PENTECOST

TOP LEFT WINDOW

PAUL'S CONVERSION

TOP RIGHT WINDOW

PETER'S ROOFTOP VISION

PENTECOST

Acts 2:1-4

Now when the day of Pentecost had come, they were all together in one place. Suddenly a sound like a

violent wind blowing came from heaven and filled the entire house where they were sitting. And

tongues spreading out like a fire appeared to them and came to rest on each one of them. All of them

were filled with the Holy Spirit, and they began to speak in other languages as the Spirit enabled them.

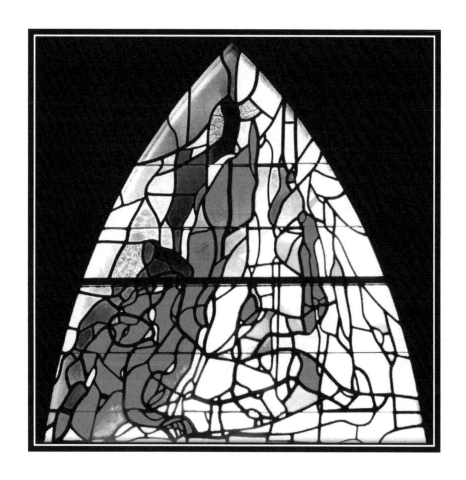

PAUL'S CONVERSION

Acts 9:1-7

Meanwhile, Saul was still breathing out murderous threats against the Lord's disciples. He went to the high priest and asked him for letters to the synagogues in Damascus, so that if he found any there who belonged to the Way, whether men or women, he might take them as prisoners to Jerusalem. As he neared Damascus on his journey, suddenly a light from heaven flashed around him. He fell to the ground and heard a voice say to him, "Saul, Saul, why do you persecute me?"

"Who are you, Lord?" Saul asked.

"I am Jesus, whom you are persecuting," he replied. "Now get up and go into the city, and you will be told what you must do."

PETER'S ROOFTOP VISION

Acts 10:9-13

About noon the following day as they were on their journey and approaching the city, Peter went up on the roof to pray. He became hungry and wanted something to eat, and while the meal was being prepared, he fell into a trance. He saw heaven opened and something like a large sheet being let down to earth by its four corners. It contained all kinds of four-footed animals, as well as reptiles and birds. Then a voice told him, "Get up, Peter. Kill and eat."

CAN YOU FIND THE RABBIT IN THE NARTHEX WINDOWS?

THE NARTHEX

EARLY INFLUENTIAL THEOLOGINS

LEFT PANEL

TOP TO BOTTOM

SEAL OF ST. AUGUSTINE OF HIPPO

SEAL OF MARTIN LUTHER

SEAL OF JOHN CALVIN

ST. AUGUSTINE OF HIPPO

After Paul one of the most widely read and influencial theologins of all time.

354-430 A.D.

HIS SEAL

A Flaming Heart Transfixed by Two Arrows

MARTIN LUTHER

Father of the Great Reformation.

1483-1546 A.D.

HIS SEAL

A Black Cross Within a Red Heart on a White Rose

JOHN CALVIN

Successor to Martin Luther as the preeminent Protestant theologin.

1509-1564 A.D.

HIS SEAL

An Outstreached Hand with a Heart

CAN YOU FIND ME IN THE SANCTUARY WINDOWS?

WHAT AM I?

THE NARTHEX

EARLY METHODISM

RIGHT SIDE PANEL

TOP TO BOTTOM

JOHN WESLEY'S COAT OF ARMS

CHARLES WESLEY'S SYMBOLS OF MUSIC

FRANCIS ASBURY ON A HORSE IN FRONT OF A
BIBLE

JOHN WESLEY

The Father of Methodism.

1703-1791 A.D.

HIS COAT OF ARMS

A Cross with Five Shells

CHARLES WESLEY

1707-1708 A.D.

MUSIC SYMBOLS

The Word "HARK"

Charles Wesley was the author of many of our Methodist hymns. The one most famous was "Hark the Herald Angles Sing" which this symbol acknowledges.

There are 65 of Charles Wesley's songs in the United Methodist Hymnal.

The Treble Clef

FRANCIS ASBURY

Francis Asbury was a circuit rider and the General Superintendent of the Methodist Societies in the United States of America in the late 1700s and early 1800s. He was responsible for the dramatic growth of Methodism during that time.

1745-1816 A.D

Asbury on a Horse in Front of a Bible

THE SANCTUARY

OLD TESTATMENT SIDE/COURTYARD

LEFT LANCET

THE PATRIARCHS

THE HAND OF GOD

THE RAM IN THE BUSH

MOSES

THE PASSOVER

JOSHUA AND HIS TRUMPET

THE HAND OF GOD

Genesis 1:26

Then God said, "Let Us make man in Our image, according to Our likeness; let them have

dominion over the fish of the sea, over the birds of the air, and over the cattle, over all

the earth and over every creeping thing that creeps on the earth."

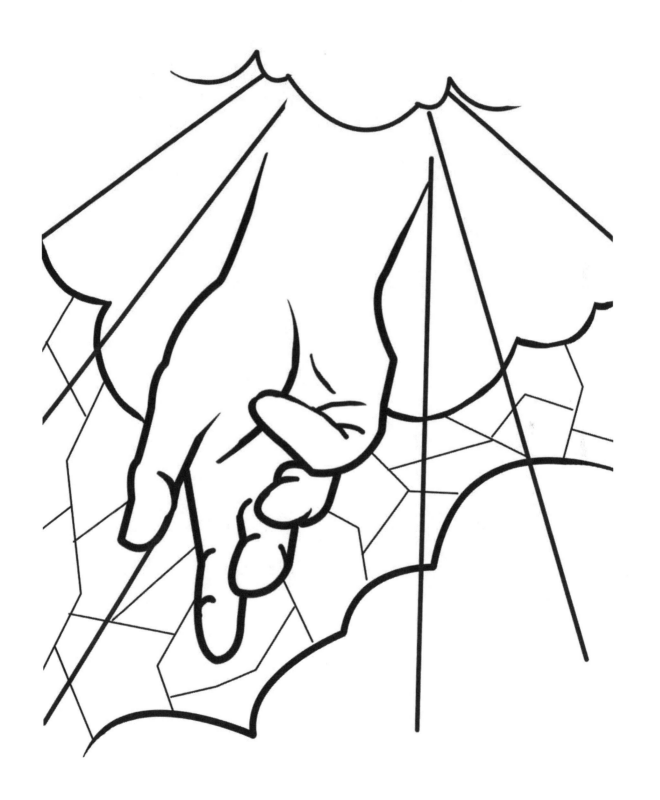

RAM IN THE BUSH

Genesis 22:11-14

And Abraham lifted up his eyes, and looked, and behold behind him a ram caught in a thicket by his horns: and Abraham went and took the ram, and offered him up for a burnt offering in the stead of his son.

MOSES AND THE TEN COMMANDMENTS

Exodus 24:12

The LORD said to Moses, "Come up to me on the mountain and stay here, and I will give you the tablets of stone with the law and commandments I have written for their instruction."

PASSOVER

Exodus 12:12-13

On that same night I will pass through Egypt and strike down every firstborn of both people and animals, and I will bring judgment on all the gods of Egypt. I am the Lord. The blood will be a sign for you on the houses where you are, and when I see the blood, I will pass over you. No destructive plague will touch you when I strike Egypt.

JOSHUA AND HIS TRUMPET

Joshua 6:20

So the people shouted when the priests blew with the trumpets: and it came to pass, when the people heard the sound of the trumpet, and the people shouted with a great shout, that the wall fell down flat, so that the people went up into the city, every man straight before him, and they took the city.

JOSHUA 6:4

Have seven priests carry trumpets of rams' horns in front of the ark. On the seventh day, march around the city seven times, with the priests blowing the trumpets.

SHOFAR

A shofar is a musical instrument of ancient origin made of a horn, traditionally that of a ram, used for Jewish religious purposes.

OLD TESTAMENT SIDE/COURTYARD

CENTER LANCET

THE PROPHETS

JESUS

THE LOCUST/AMOS

ISAIAH

THE RAINBOW COVENANT

DANIEL AND THE LIONS

JONAH AND THE WHALE

JESUS THE PROPHET

Mathew 21:11

And the multitude said this is Jesus the prophet of Nazareth of Galilee.

THE LOCUST

Amos 7:1-3

Thus the Lord GOD showed me: Behold, He formed locust swarms at the beginning of the late crop; indeed it was the late crop after the king's mowings. And so it was, when they had finished eating the grass of the land, that I said:"O Lord GOD, forgive, I pray! Oh, that Jacob may stand, For he is small!"

So the LORD relented concerning this. "It shall not be," said the LORD.

ISAIAH

Isaiah 53:5

But he was wounded for our transgressions, he was bruised for our iniquities; upon him

was the chastisement that made us whole, and with his stripes we are healed.

THE RAINBOW COVENANT

Genesis 9:15-17

And I will remember my covenant, which is between me and you and every living creature of all flesh; and the waters shall no more become a flood to destroy all flesh. And the bow shall be in the cloud; and I will look on it, that I may remember the everlasting covenant between God and every living creature of all flesh that is on the earth. And God said to Noah, This is the token of the covenant, which I have established between me and all the flesh that is on earth.

DANIEL AND THE LIONS

Daniel 6:22

"My God sent his angel and he shut the mouths of the lions. They have not hurt me, because I was found innocent in his sight. Nor have I ever done any wrong before you, O king."

JONAH AND THE WHALE

Jonah 1:17

Now the LORD had prepared a great fish to swallow up Jonah. And Jonah was in the belly of the fish three days and three nights.

WHERE IS TARSHISH?

WHY WAS JONAH GOING THERE?

WHO ARE SHADRACH, MESHACH, AND ABEDNEGO?

WHAT DID GOD TELL NOAH ABOUT THE RAINBOW?

OLD TESTAMENT SIDE/COURTYARD

RIGHT LANCET

THE KINGS

THE COMPLETED TEMPLE

DAVID AND HIS HARP

SOLOMON AND THE SCALES OF JUSTICE

THE COMPLETED TEMPLE

1 Chronicles 22:19

Now devote your heart and soul to seeking the LORD your God. Begin to build the sanctuary of the LORD God, so that you may bring the ark of the covenant of the LORD and the sacred articles belonging to God into the temple that will be built for the Name of the LORD.

KING SOLOMON

1 kings 3:25-27

The king said, "Divide the living child in two, and give half to the one and half to the other." Then the woman whose child was the living one spoke to the king, for she was deeply stirred over her son and said, "Oh, my lord, give her the living child, and by no means kill him." But the other said, "He shall be neither mine nor yours; divide him!" Then the king said, "Give the first woman the living child, and by no means kill him. She is his mother."

DAVID AND HIS HARP

1 Samuel 16:23

And whenever the tormenting spirit from God troubled Saul, David would play the harp.

Then Saul would feel better, and the tormenting spirit would go away.

NEW TESTAMENT SIDE/LAKE

LEFT LANCET

EARLY MINISTRY OF JESUS

THE BABY JESUS AND THE MANGER

JESUS CALLING THE DISCIPLES

THE DOVE AND WATER FROM A SHELL

(SYMBOLS OF BAPTISM AND THE HOLY SPIRIT)

BABY JESUS IN THE MANGER

Luke 2:7

And she brought forth her firstborn Son, and wrapped Him in swaddling cloths, and laid

Him in a manger, because there was no room for them in the inn.

JESUS CALLING THE DISCIPLES

Mathew 4:18-20

As Jesus was walking beside the Sea of Galilee, he saw two brothers, Simon called Peter and his brother Andrew. They were casting a net into the lake, for they were fishermen. "Come, follow me," Jesus said, "and I will send you out to fish for people." At once they left their nets and followed him.

WATER AND THE DOVE-BAPTISM AND THE HOLY SPIRIT

Mathew 3:16

As soon as Jesus was baptized, he went up out of the water. At that moment heaven was

opened, and he saw the Spirit of God descending like a dove and alighting on him.

CAN YOU FIND ME IN THE WINDOWS?

NEW TESTAMENT SIDE/LAKE

CENTER LANCET

LIFE OF JESUS ON EARTH

JESUS ASCENDED TO HEAVEN

THE SYMBOLS OF THE CROSS

THE PHOENIX

THE LAST SUPPER

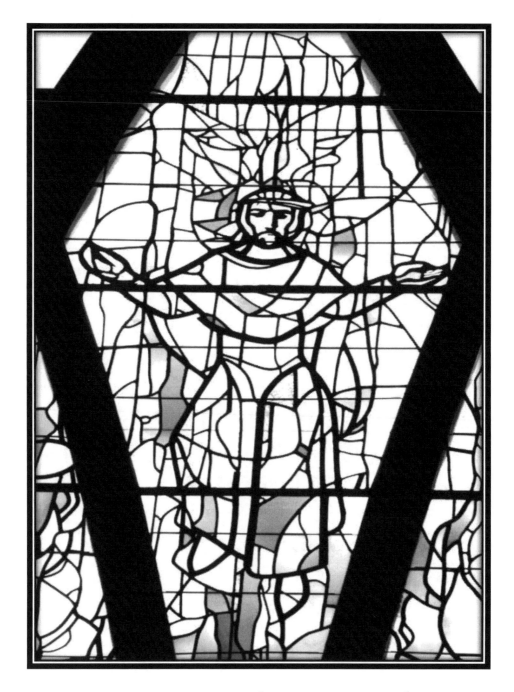

JESUS ASCENDED TO HEAVEN AND CROWNED AS KING

Mark 16:19

So then after the Lord had spoken unto them, he was received up into heaven, and sat

on the right hand of God.

THE CROSS AND SYMBOLS OF THE CRUCIFIXION

Mark 15:20

And when they had mocked him, they took off the purple robe and put his own clothes on him. Then they led him out to crucify him.

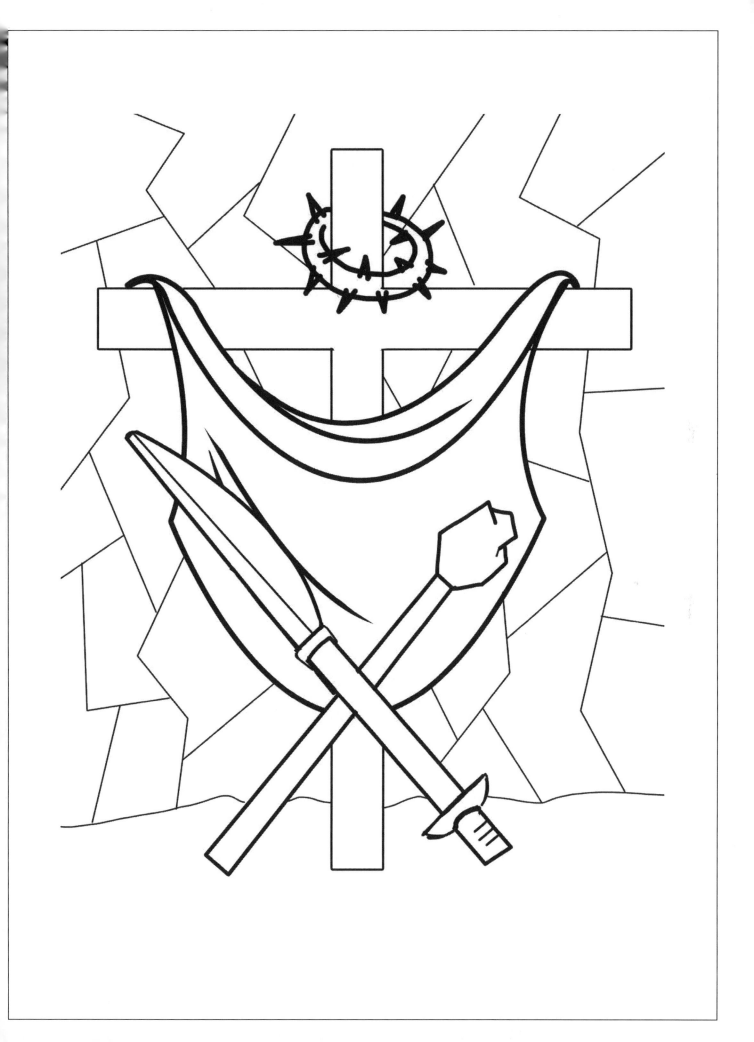

THE PHOENIX SYMBOL OF THE RESURRECTION OF JESUS

The mythical Phoenix is said to have built a nest, set it on fire and then to have risen from the ashes in victory. The Phoenix has become symbolic of the resurrection, immortality and the life-after-death of Jesus.

THE LAST SUPPER

Luke 22:14-22

When the hour came, Jesus and his apostles reclined at the table. And he said to them, "I have eagerly desired to eat this Passover with you before I suffer. For I tell you, I will not eat it again until it finds fulfillment in the kingdom of God." After taking the cup, he gave thanks and said, "Take this and divide it among you. For I tell you I will not drink again of the fruit of the vine until the kingdom of God comes." And he took bread, gave thanks and broke it, and gave it to them, saying, "This is my body given for you; do this in remembrance of me." In the same way, after the supper he took the cup, saying, "This cup is the new covenant in my blood, which is poured out for you."

CAN YOU FIND ME IN THE WINDOWS?

IS THAT SMOKE?

NEW TESTAMENT SIDE/LAKE

RIGHT LANCET

THE MIRACLES

THE LAMB AND THE ROD AND STAFF

THE MIRACLE AT CANA

THE HEALING OF THE BLEEDING WOMAN

JESUS PREACHING FROM A BOAT

THE LAMB AND THE ROD AND STAFF

John 10:11

I am the good shepherd. The good shepherd lays down his life for the sheep.

THE WEDDING AT CANA-WATER TO WINE MIRACLE

John 2:1-4

And the third day there was a marriage in Cana of Galilee; and the mother of Jesus was

there. And both Jesus was called, and his disciples, to the marriage. And when they

wanted wine, the mother of Jesus saith unto him, They have no wine. Jesus saith unto

her, Woman, what have I to do with thee? Mine hour is not yet come.

THE BLEEDING WOMAN OF FAITH

Mark 5:24-29

And a certain woman, which had an issue of blood twelve years, and had suffered many things of many physicians, and had spent all that she had, and was nothing bettered, but rather grew worse. When she had heard of Jesus, came in the press behind, and touched his garment. For she said, if I may touch but his clothes, I shall be whole. And straightway the fountain of her blood was dried up; and she felt in her body that she was healed of that plague.

JESUS PREACHING FROM THE BOAT

Mark 3:5-9

Jesus withdrew with his disciples to the lake, and a large crowd from Galilee followed. When they heard about all he was doing, many people came to him from Judea, Jerusalem, Idumea, and the regions across the Jordan and around Tyre and Sidon. Because of the crowd he told his disciples to have a small boat ready for him, to keep the people from crowding him.

DOOR LIGHTS OF NARTHEX AND SACTUARY

NARTHEX

ANGELS OF PRAISE AND ACTS OF MERCY

FAR LEFT NARTHEX DOOR LIGHT

ANGEL OF PRAISE WITH CENSER

CENTER NARTHEX DOOR LIGHTS

LEFT- LOAVES OF BREAD

RIGHT- LAMP SHINING BRIGHTLY

FAR RIGHT NARTHEX DOOR LIGHT

ANGEL OF PRAISE AND TRUMPET

SANCUARY

OLD TESTAMENT DOORS (COURTYARD)

LEFT DOOR LIGHT

NOAH AND THE ARK

RIGHT DOOR LIGHT

THE GOOD SHEPHERD

RIGHT ALTAR DOOR LIGHT/LEFT ALTAR DOOR LIGHT

JOY, VARIETY AND COLOR OF CREATION

AS DESCRIBED IN THE PSALMS

NARTHEX FAR LEFT DOOR LIGHT

ANGEL OF PRAISE WITH A CENSER

CENSER: A CONTAINER IN WHICH INCENSE IS BURNED

THE CENSER

LEVITICUS 16:12

He is to take a censer full of burning coals from the altar before the LORD and two handfuls of finely ground fragrant incense and take them behind the curtain.

PSALM 141:1-2

I call to you, LORD, come quickly to me;
hear me when I call to you.
May my prayer be set before you like incense;
may the lifting up of my hands be like the evening sacrifice.

REVELATION 5:8

And when he had taken it, the four living creatures and the twenty-four elders fell down before the Lamb. Each one had a harp and they were holding golden bowls full of incense, which are the prayers of God's people.

REVELATION 8:3-5

Another angel, who had a golden censer, came and stood at the altar. He was given much incense to offer, with the prayers of all God's people, on the golden altar in front of the throne. The smoke of the incense, together with the prayers of God's people, went up before God from the angel's hand. Then the angel took the censer, filled it with fire from the altar, and hurled it on the earth; and there came peals of thunder, rumblings, flashes of lightning and an earthquake.

The censer is a container, usually with a closed top, containing hot charcoal that is used to burn incense. (Incense is derived from the Latin word *incensum* or to set on fire.) Frankincense and myrrh are common substances used for incense because of the strong and aromatic smoke produced when they burn. The smoke of burning incense is interpreted as a symbol of the prayer of the faithful rising to heaven and symbolic of giving a pleasing sacrifice to the Lord.

CENTER NARTHEX DOOR/ LEFT LIGHT

BASKET OF LOAVES AND TWO FISH

WATER POURING INTO CUP

THE SERAPE(BLANKETLIKE SHAWL) AND SANDALS

NARTHEX CENTER DOORS

LEFT DOOR LIGHT SYMBOLISM

TOP TO BOTTOM

MATTHEW 14:19-21

And he directed the people to sit down on the grass. Taking the five loaves and the two fish and looking up to heaven, he gave thanks and broke the loaves. Then he gave them to the people. They all ate and were satisfied, and the disciples picked up twelve basketfuls of broken pieces that were left over. The number of those who ate was about five thousand men, besides women and children.

Basket of loaves and two fish not only to recall the feeding of the multitude, but to remind us to feed our hungry brothers and sisters.

Water poured from a jug into a cup emphasizes giving drink to the thirsty. The window also reminds us to consider and use water as one of our precious gifts.

The serape and the sandals tell us to clothe the naked and to be aware of how others often live without the necessities of life.

CENTER NARTHEX DOOR /RIGHT LIGHT

LAMP SHINING BRIGHTLY

OLIVE BRANCHS/FLAGON POURING OIL

SMALL ROOM AND CANDLE ON A TABLE

PRISON DOOR WITH KEY

NARTHEX CENTER DOORS

RIGHT DOOR LIGHT SYMBOLISM

TOP TO BOTTOM

MATTHEW 7:15-20

"Beware of false prophets, who come to you in sheep's clothing, but inwardly they are ravenous wolves. You will know them by their fruits. Do men gather grapes from thorn bushes or figs from thistles? Even so, every good tree bears good fruit, but a bad tree bears bad fruit. A good tree cannot bear bad fruit, nor can a bad tree bear good fruit. Every tree that does not bear good fruit is cut down and thrown into the fire. Therefore by their fruits you will know them."

A lamp shining brightly signifies the soul alive with grace and charity.

Olive branches and a small flagon pouring oil are both symbols of healing. Roses are represented to emphasize the sweet unction of visiting and comforting the sick.

A small room is seen at the bottom with a table upon which a candle burns smybolizing hospitality in welcoming of the stranger and the homeless, for in doing so, we welcome Christ Himself.

A prison door with a key invites us to visit the "imprisoned" both in the literal and figurative sense of the word.

"By their fruits you will know them."

NARTHEX

FAR RIGHT DOOR LIGHT

ANGEL OF PRAISE AND TRUMPET

THE TRUMPET

NUMBERS 10:1-7

The LORD said to Moses: "Make two trumpets of hammered silver, and use them for calling the community together and for having the camps set out. When both are sounded, the whole community is to assemble before you at the entrance to the tent of meeting. If only one is sounded, the leaders—the heads of the clans of Israel—are to assemble before you. When a trumpet blast is sounded, the tribes camping on the east are to set out. At the sounding of a second blast, the camps on the south are to set out. The blast will be the signal for setting out. To gather the assembly, blow the trumpets, but not with the signal for setting out.

JOSHUA 6:4-5

Have seven priests carry trumpets of rams' horns in front of the ark. On the seventh day, march around the city seven times, with the priests blowing the trumpets. When you hear them sound a long blast on the trumpets, have the whole army give a loud shout; then the wall of the city will collapse and the army will go up, everyone straight in."

MATTHEW 24:31

And he will send his angels with a loud trumpet call, and they will gather his elect from the four winds, from one end of the heavens to the other.

REVELATION 8:2

And I saw the seven angels who stand before God, and seven trumpets were given to them.

REVELATION 11:15

The seventh angel sounded his trumpet, and there were loud voices in heaven, which said: "The kingdom of the world has become the kingdom of our Lord and of his Messiah, and he will reign forever and ever."

SANCTUARY

OLD TESTAMENT SIDE

RIGHT DOOR LIGHT

THE GOOD SHEPHERD AND HIS SHEEP

THE GOOD SHEPHERD

PSALM 23

My shepherd is the Lord; there is nothing I shall want.

The Good Shepherd is represented lovingly tending his sheep. One is carried on his shoulder and another stands at his feet.

SANCTUARY

OLD TESTAMENT SIDE

LEFT DOOR LIGHT

NOAH'S ARK

NOAH AND THE ARK

GENESIS 8:11

The dove returned to him in the evening, but in its beak there was an olive leaf that it had plucked! So Noah knew that the flood waters had decreased on the land.

Depicted in this door light is Noah on the deck of the ark waiting for the return of the dove with the olive branch. You see at the top the dove and branch, in the middle the Ark and a fish with waves of the ocean at the bottom.

DO YOU SEE NOAH ON THE DECK OF THE ARK?

SANCTUARY

RIGHT ALTER DOOR LIGHT

JOY, VARIETY, AND COLOR OF CREATION

PSALMS: 96,145,147,148.

DOOR LIGHTS TO THE RIGHT AND LEFT OF THE ALTAR

The two door lights on each side of the altar are meant to suggest the joy, infinite variety, and color found throughout creation as praised by the psalmist.

Psalm 96: *Oh sing to the Lord a new song all the earth. Declare his glory among nations.*

Psalm 145: *All your works shall give thanks to You, O Lord, and all your faithful shall bless you.*

Psalm 147: *Make melody to god on the lyre, He covers the heavens with clouds, Prepares rain for the earth. He makes his wind blow and the waters flow.*

Psalm 148: *Praise the Lord from the earth, you sea monsters and all deeps, Fire and hail, snow and frost, Mountains and all hills, fruit trees and all cedars, Wild animals and all cattle, Creeping things and flying birds...*

The left door light specifically shows radiant light spilling from the top of the window. Warm flower and fruit-like blossoms signifying the generativity of God's creative love and the fruits of the earth. The deep blue green at the bottom symbolizes water which nourishes all of lift.

SANCTUARY

LEFT ALTAR DOOR LIGHT

RADIANT LIGHT/FLOWER AND FRUIT

WATER THAT NOURISHES ALL OF LIFE

Where did the stained glass studio leave their mark?

Narthex Entrance/Right panel/Below Francis Asbury

(Man on a horse)

February 2014

Jennie Cooper Press

660 A Lanier Park Dr.

Suite A

Gainesville, Ga.

Special thanks to Willet Stained Glass Studios of Philadelphia, Pa.

for providing the interpretation of the figures in the stained glass.

Created by

John McHugh

Photography

John McHugh

Illustrations

Taryn Dufault

Karen McHugh